# THE COST OF THE WIN I

## Reflections of My Journey and What It Cost to Win

*Tamara Lofton*

authorHOUSE®

*AuthorHouse™*
*1663 Liberty Drive*
*Bloomington, IN 47403*
*www.authorhouse.com*
*Phone: 1 (800) 839-8640*



*Published by AuthorHouse 12/20/2018*

*ISBN: 978-1-5462-7332-5 (sc)*
*ISBN: 978-1-5462-7331-8 (e)*

*Library of Congress Control Number: 2018914969*

*Print information available on the last page.*

*Background Research:*
*Dictionary.Com/Thesaurus.Com*

*Vines Concise Dictionary of Bible Words*
*W.E. Vine, Thomas Nelson Publishers 1985, 1980*

*Vines Complete Expository Dictionary*
*W.E. Vine, Merrill F. Unger, William White Jr.*
*Thomas Nelson Publisher 1968,1980,1985,1996*

*King James Bible Commentary*
*Thomas Nelson Publisher 1983, 1999*

*Athletic Resource Information:*
*Competing and Being Part of the Games*
*https://secure.registration.olympic.org/en/faq/category/detail/11*
*Conditioning Exercises:*
*Live Strong.Com/go4life.nia.nih.gov/www.captel.com/2013*
*Sports Medicine_News-Science Daily*
*www.sciencedaily.com/news/health_medicine/sports_medicine/*

## Reflections

"The Cost of the Win" is an inspiring compilation of life experiences and tools that can be used to help you journey well and finish on top! This book can help you to make the necessary "Adjustments" and gain "Courage" to understand that though you may have "Some Dark Mornings, it's Still Morning"
Evang. Tammy Lindsay, Wilmington, DE

"Public Display vs Private Preparation"...I had to take my time and listen to this chapter. The writing is clear and thought provoking. I find it effective for the new convert as well as the seasoned believer. I can't wait for the release of this project!!!
Psalmist Deborah Thomas, Memphis, TN

"Some Mornings are Darker Than Others, but it's Still Morning" left me with only one thought... "Morning is only one minute away from midnight!!!"
Dr. Beatrice Gardiner,
Rehoboth Outreach Christian Center, Dallas, TX

At first glance, the title of Chapter 6 caught my attention. Then the quote by James Lee Griffin, "Morning is the mystery to the beginning of infinity" resonated within me…
Dr. D'Ann Johnson, New Covenant Ministries, Lithonia, GA

# Dedication

It takes a village to raise a child…
It takes a village to shape by example..
It takes a village to promote good character…
It takes a village to stabilize integrity…..
It takes a village to produce a leader….

To the "Village"…..
Willie M. Strong(Madea), Mr. James Lee Griffin Sr.,
Deacon Leonia & Eld. Beverly Jones,
Pastor Ulysses Purdy,
Bishop G.E. Patterson,
Apostle Gail Patterson, Ms. Love Bowie,
Bishop J.D. & Lisa V. Wiley-Taylor,
Mrs. Carrie Tigler,
Prophet Wilbert & Debra Ayres,
Apostle Bill & Dr. D'Ann Johnson,
Eld. Gordan Graham, Eld. Theresa Gilstrap,
Pastor Fred & Margaret Caldwell,
Dr. Winton & Eld. Lavern Robinson,
Dr. Toni Alvarado, Apostle Richard D. Henton,
Rev. Victor Belton…

These eagles shaped my life and taught me to soar.
Although bruised along the way, they displayed
their scars as trophies of honor. Consistently
engaging in the good fight of faith, they realized
that "winners never quit and quitters never win".

They recognized His voice,
responded to His call,
and responsibly completed each ordained assignment,
teaching me to do the same....

## Mantra, Mission, and Message

*I shall pass through this world but once.*
*Any good therefore that I can do*
*or any kindness that I can show to any human being,*
*let me do it now.*

*Let me not defer nor neglect it,*
*for I shall not pass this way again.*

*Each day has one thing in common with the next.*
*Both offer opportunities to show kindness,*
*and when missed, those opportunities*
*leave you with unwanted regrets.*

*Stephen Grellet 1855*

# Contents

Introduction .......... xv

Chapter 1 Prelude .......... 1

Chapter 2 Adjustments .......... 4

Chapter 3 Courage .......... 7

Chapter 4 Public Display vs Private Preparation .......... 12

Chapter 5 Treat Impatience with Patience .......... 17

Chapter 6 Some Mornings are Darker Than Others but It's Still Morning .......... 22

Chapter 7 Listen to the Leading .......... 28

Chapter 8 Conditioning .......... 33

Summary .......... 37

# Introduction

While viewing many disturbing news reports, I became overwhelmed. Several high-profile athletes and media personalities were being exposed for illegal activities. I labored with the idea, that the goal to just win first place, was not the only beneficial, valuable, exceptional, distinguished, phenomenal, or honorable prize.

The challenge to triumph, in all of life's arenas, calls for a well-rounded individual. Integrity, character, responsibility, and accountability, yoked with preparation, practice, procedure, and performance, configures the proper foundation. This successful winner now possesses the ability to maintain the achievement.

There is a cost attached to every win! The price paid, the experience gained, the lesson learned, and the completion of the journey, is the most essential distinction one could ever attain. A grace will follow with seasoned maturity and a motive that is equitable.

# Chapter I
# PRELUDE

The major portion of my early adolescence was quite awkward. I enjoyed ballet, and was quite proficient at it, but being overweight, prevented moving to the next level; toe shoes. Modeling was also fun, but age appropriate clothes back then, did not cater to a plus sized pre-teen. The desire to be in front of any type of camera as an actress, talk show host, comedian, or athlete was merely a fleeting wish.

Academically, I earned good grades, but always found myself a few points away from being top student. In High School, I was very shy, not popular at all, and had few friends. Political pursuits, whether campaigning for a class office or a public service job, were definitely out of the question. With science being my least favorite subject, and a bit queasy at the sight of blood, all aspirations of becoming a doctor or nurse, were totally out of the career spectrum.

Consequently, I immersed myself in analytical thinking. Never taking anything at face value, I questioned everything that crossed my path. Rarely verbalizing what was really going on in my head, I conditioned myself to internalize my thoughts. I just wouldn't speak in front of others.

Life as I knew back then, really didn't make sense. The things that I saw were so confusing:

- The inconsistent reactions to everyday life…
- The inconsiderate responses of my peers….
- The habitual, traditions of mediocre individuals who expected me to embrace that foolishness just because….

I did have music in my genes, and a Hammond B-3 Organ that I could express myself through. That was my catalyst, my incentive, my motivation, to break the cycle, and to make a difference in this world.

And then, the light bulb came on!

- the intuition
- the observation
- the understanding
- the vision
- the wisdom
- the discernment

The comprehension emerged from my spirit that asking questions is a part of the learning process. The power of choice is a special gift from God. I am totally responsible for my choices in life. It is ok to be human; I am not wonder woman. Being saved enhances the real me. I now have Him to lead, guide, and direct me through life's process. Winning 1st place is not the only prize of value. There is a cost, a price, a sacrifice, a purpose attached to every win!

*"From Challenge to Victory"*

*Challenges, Trouble, Trials, and Tests*
*Obstacles, Hindrances, Road Blocks,*
*What's next?*

*Detours and Sidetracks assigned to your life,*
*Assigned to your route, course, and path,*
*Such a Fight!*

*Without a test there would be no fight!*
*Without a fight there could be no battle!*
*With no official battle, there can be no victory!*
*To void the victory, would never yield a conquest!*
*Without a conquest, there can be no possession!*

*Fight, Possess, and Win!*

## Chapter II
# ADJUSTMENTS

change of position, harmony achieved by modification,
adaption, alteration, arrangement, acclimation,
correcting or conformance to a
particular condition or purpose

*The king's heart is a stream of water in the hand of the Lord;
He turns it wherever He will (Proverbs 22:1)*

*"The trigger to solutions that change
situations and circumstances."*

*Athletes and dancers correct their form to heighten their skill level. They practice frequently, making appropriate corrections, until the execution is flawless. For three years, they participate in several World Championship competitions. Eventually, the pre-qualifying scores afford them the opportunity to compete in subsequent trials. The ultimate goal is to qualify for the International Olympic Team.*

My most memorable encounter with adjustments came shortly after accepting an opportunity to travel as a musician for an evangelist. I thought that I would be playing for two services per day (12 noon and 7:30pm). The rest of the down time would be left for "sightseeing and rest and relaxation." Reality quickly set in. My daily tasks turned into more than ten hour days as I served as driver, valet, administrator, travel agent, conference coordinator, bible teacher, sermonic narrator, musician, and more.

At first, I was a little reluctant, but as I began to yield to the progressive demands of ministry, transformation took place. I realized that I had capabilities in areas that I had never pursued. Presently surprised, I completed each new task with proficiency and excellence. And in reflection, I enjoyed the work.

Making adjustments are now very intriguing to me. I embrace them as dear friends. These steps, have been the door to numerous growth opportunities. I've lived in six states, pursued seven careers, and now at sixty-four, I have still another career pursuit in my view. The adjustments were not always comfortable or easy but the reward far outweighed the *modification* demands.

Did this series of changes cost me something? Yes, family, friends, familiar surroundings, close relationships, comfort, birthday celebrations, social activities, and much more. But did I win? Most definitely! I've won favor, insight, capabilities, and experience.

**Make the Adjustment to Win….!**

*You are not a Thermometer;*
*an instrument that merely registers the temperature.*

*You are a Thermostat;*
*the device that automatically adjusts the temperature*
*to a desired level.*

*Living things grow!*
*Growing things change!*

*You have been called to set the tone,*
*formulate the atmosphere,*
*orchestrate the mood,*
*maintain the temperature!*

*You are the example.*
*You are the "Instrument of Change".*

*If it does not exist,*
*then You must create it to be!*

# Chapter III
# COURAGE

bravery, audacity, determination, endurance,
fortitude, grit, spunk, tenacity,
backbone, guts, stoutheartedness

*God has not given us the spirit of fear*
*but of power, love, and a sound mind (II Timothy 1:7)*

*"A courage to stand,*
*A courage to endure,*
*A courage that is reckless, empowering and sure.*
*Tenacity, audacity, gallantry, and guts,*
*Be thou strong and very courageous.*
*Assume the posture, no if ands or buts!"*

*The courage of an athlete supersedes their ability to merely perform. In the midst of physical pain and multiple injuries, they must continue to play the game with tenacity and determination. With triumphant wins, and memories of past defeat, they must immediately focus, clothe themselves in courage, and persevere to win.*

In 1990, I needed surgery. At the time, I resided in Mississippi, but chose to have the surgery in Atlanta. My Georgia family would be the only support system during the recovery process. While engaged in the pre-op consultation process, a suggestion was made to have some plasma on hand in case of excessive bleeding. My blood type was O positive. This didn't match with my maternal side of the family who all had B blood types. At that time, I had no information concerning my father, nor his medical history.

There was an option to donate my own blood in advance, but I was severely anemic. With the surgery date quickly approaching, there just wasn't enough time to safely give blood, allow my system to replenish itself, and still remain strong enough for the upcoming surgery. Added to this dilemma, was a far more serious matter. The existing blood supply had been tainted by the Aids virus. The Red Cross stated that the present blood supply had gone through a purifying process, but they couldn't promise that it was totally safe. If I began to lose blood during surgery, they would have to use the plasma that was presently on hand. I needed an O Positive Donor immediately!

*I will answer them before they even call to me.*
*While they are still talking about their needs,*
*I will go ahead and answer their prayers!*
*(Isaiah 65:24 NLT)*

Of course, God knew all of the details way before I became aware of these upcoming events. He orchestrated this entire encounter and I watched as He unfolded every minute detail.

Approximately seventeen years prior, in the early 1970's, I moved to Memphis to finish college. This was my first time away from home, but I embraced the challenge with great expectancy. While there, I prayed for, and welcomed new relationships into my life. A family in the church took me under their watchful wing. I didn't know them and they didn't know me but we bonded. Within a few months, a spiritual adoption took place. They became an extension of my biological family and I gained a new sister. I lived in Memphis for eleven years and never once had we discussed any medical history, or blood types. I didn't even know what my blood type was back then.

My Memphis family relocated to Atlanta several years prior to my medical dilemma. While sharing my concerns, as the Lord would have it, my Memphis sister had the solution to this compelling challenge. Before verbalizing my thoughts she said, "I'm O positive, I can give you some blood".

I always called her my twin sister because we were so much alike. We were a perfect match! She donated willingly. The surgery was a success and I didn't need the transfusion after all. My initial courage to share my concerns, blessed another patient with anointed, untainted, pints of blood.

The majority of my geographical moves began without knowing anyone in the destination city. With an unction from God, and no family or friends, I moved with great expectation that He would place the right people on my route. With every move, the Lord placed me in a loving, spiritually mature, and bible based church. They became my family. With each new learning experience, the assignment was established and I progressed in the direction of my ordained calling of God. Was I nervous and a little scared? Most definitely, but I began to actively practice, II Timothy 1:7, and then courage was established. With this sound wisdom tool, the journey became easier, and the transitions more bearable.

**Apply Courage To Win!**

*Practice makes improvement.*

*Improvement strengthens the ability.*

*Consistent and improved ability produces maturity.*

*Continuous maturity breeds excellence.*

*Completed excellence produces perfection!*

## Chaper IV

# PUBLIC DISPLAY VS PRIVATE PREPARATION

personal, confidential,
exclusive, secret, behind the scenes

*Prepare your outside work, make it fit for yourself in the field,*
*And afterward, build your house (Proverbs 24:27 NKJ)*

*"Preparation is a safeguard, a precaution, and a plan,*
*That will train, alert, and mold you,*
*while pursuing His divine plan.*

*Construction, and formation, education, expectation,*
*reinforced determination, as you build on a solid foundation."*

*The public display of an accomplished runner is exciting and invigorating. Very seldom does the spectator think about the exhaustive training regiment, qualifying time constraints, proper diet, approved attire, and the rest and recovery demanded upon each individual team member. The hours of private preparation far exceed the glorious exhibition of the actual race.*

As a rising juvenile pianists, I must admit that I didn't like to practice very much. My very watchful and wise piano teacher noticed early on that I would listen to my sister practice, then mimic the melody enough to master the musical pieces given to her. Eventually, my teacher changed her game plan by scheduling our weekly lessons on different days. Then she strategically assigned us totally different musical selections. I would be left to figure out the beats, and painstakingly work out the necessary skills, all on my own. I must say, this was indeed a challenge, but I learned to figure it out, became disciplined, and a better musician in the process.

The issue of private preparation yielding excellence was birthed, and became a permanent fixture in my musicality for years to come. In fact, I am hesitant to take on a job of any kind without engaging myself in the proficient private prep needed to execute the task assigned to me. Who would've known that a simple adjustment of a piano lesson would impact my entire life and shape my destiny.... "despise not the days of small beginning" (Zechariah 4:10).

**Excellence is the Standard... Practice is the Vehicle!**

Delectable gourmet meals begin with food prep: picking greens, cutting vegetables, brimming chicken, marinating steaks, gutting and scaling fish, and much more. Before the feast comes the labor. Before becoming a part of the team, comes skill development and performance qualifications. Before performing in the concert, comes many hours of personal practice and weekly group rehearsals. Before the law student qualifies for the Bar exam many hours of research are required to support arguments that will convict or acquit potential clients before a jury.

How many times have you heard someone say, "I wish that I could be them"; a concert pianist, a well-known rapper, a professional athlete, a gold medal recipient, the winner of the Nobel Peace Prize, or an anointed preacher of the gospel.

**"To be, you must do!"**

The real work is in the prep. You must labor, and sacrifice to achieve proficiency in your area of expertise. The bible says what is done in secret, will be rewarded openly (Matthew 6:1-4). Many aspire public accolades and visible acknowledgements, but refuse to do the labor required behind the scenes…

Of much is given, much is required (Luke 12:36).

Private preparation has served as a launching pad, conditioning me for service. An intentional daily prayer time, enhanced with frequent fasting, were also required. The stability of the word of truth has tempered my attitude, and established my character. The discipline to study, and the ability to focus, has developed an attention span not easily distracted. Embracing maturity, and grasping the distinction between ego and confidence, I can now handle the promotion that only comes from God.

When I accepted Christ as Savior and Lord of my life, I asked for only three things: To help me to stay in His will always, to apply wisdom to every situation, and for patience.

Back then, I didn't realize the gravity and depth of my request. He has indeed answered these requests with the opportunity for more work that requires even more private preparation!

**Win in Private to Prepare for Public Promotion!**

*My attitude influences my mindset.*

*My mindset determines my approach.*

*My approach has the potential*
*to settle a dispute.*

*or*

*To completely dismantle*
*a peaceful solution.*

Chapter V

# TREAT IMPATIENCE WITH PATIENCE

deal with, examine, cure, correct,
kick the habit, medicate, minister to, rehabilitate

*But let patience have her perfect work,*
*that ye may be perfect and entire*
*wanting nothing (James 1:4-8).*

*"Patience is the companion of wisdom."*
*St. Augustine 354A.D.-430 A.D.*

*When an athlete is injured, the doctor begins with an intense patient consultation. Based on the feedback given, they order a battery of tests which will confirm or deny the presence of the malady. When the test results are confirmed, the doctor then prescribes a plan that the athlete can follow. This plan has the possibility to totally cure the injury or to manage the symptoms through treatment. Medication, therapy, a lifestyle change, or as a last resort, surgery, are then suggested. Now a major consideration, to comply with the present evaluation, must be agreed upon. The healing process will not be successful if the patient chooses not to follow the regiment, or adhere to the doctor's orders.*

I remember my first life altering encounter with patience. It was my senior year, the final semester of college. Three weeks into the semester, I found out that there was one education course that I needed to graduate. Somehow, this important fact was missed during the registration process, three weeks prior. This course was only offered once per year. My advisor quickly assisted me with special admission to this class and the academic year preceded as planned.

The stress of locating the required text book, and making up missed assignments, thrust me into anxiety mode. Added to that stress, was the challenge of student teaching on two academic levels; elementary and secondary, the removal of three wisdom teeth at the same time, by an oral surgeon, serving as minister of music for a very progressive church, and the focus of a very demanding mother, who ran my life long distance from Illinois. At that time we didn't have email or the ability to text, "Thank God", only the telephone!

I became very depressed and hadn't learned how to release any of my burdens to the Lord. Nor had I learned to "cast "or merely throw my cares in His direction. I was tormented, distraught, crying, and about to drive my car into a wooded area adjacent to the Memphis Zoo.

There is no temptation taken you, but
such as is common to man.

But God with the temptation provides
also a way of escape,
that you may bear it (I Corinthian 10:13).

At that exact moment, a song began to play on the radio by Timothy Wright. The lyrics ministering to me, "I give my heart, I give my mind, I give my all to Him…. everything, everything." For the first time in my life I gave everything to the Lord that was bothering me, and a peace came over me that I had never felt before. I surrendered my life all over again, Memphis State, the stress of demanding classes and assignments, the busy rehearsal schedule at church, the lingering discomfort of oral surgery, and my demanding mother. The spirit of the Lord, through that song, stopped me from killing myself that day. Yes, I was "saved and sanctified" as the saints say, but my impatient way of trying to fix my own situation, disturbed the peace that I should've been walking in. If I hadn't surrendered the overwhelming state that I was in that day, I may not have been here to share this testimony with all of you.

Patience is an applied treasure; a verb, an action, a response. It is not a lifeless picture, mounted on a canvass, or a brilliant memento, polished and glistening, from an elaborate trophy case. It is not a casual word injected into a common discussion between friends while desiring a mansion or luxury car that will not fit into their present budget.

Patience is a result of trauma, tragedy, and suffering. Patience is the calm that comes after a traumatic storm. Patience is the feedback that results from your inner spirit when you've done everything that you know to do, while trying to fix a situation, and it still doesn't end the way you thought it should. Patience is standing in agreement with His word, and accepting His will over yours, in every situation. Then, pursue the next assignment with joy and anticipation.

I recall being eighteen, ambitious, newly saved, zealous, and eager to please God in every way. In my ignorance, not willful, nor intentional, but plainly a lack of undeveloped discernment, I asked Him to give me patience. The full weight of this request would be walked out over many years of tolerance, endurance, long-suffering, understanding, persistence, and perseverance.

Many hours of instruction, grueling assignments, pop quizzes, and make up tests, have engaged and reinforced this one topic in my life. The knowledge of patience is permanently branded in my brain. The application of patience is a permanent resident of my inner core.

I cherish the observant glances and respectful remarks of my peers. I smile in reflection to the journey that I've traveled, with a purposeful intent to always reach a peaceful destination. I eagerly embrace the teachings of the bible and stand in agreement with every anointed word. But in practice, I still experience a great challenge to be as patient with myself as I am with others.

The sickness has already been evaluated.<br>
The diagnosis is also sure.<br>
The illness is impatience,<br>
and there is only one cure!

**Win, While You Wait, in Patience!**

***A Cooperative Response***

*To live, to love, and then receive,*
*achieve success and grow.*
*Develop fully in His word,*
*Together we can flow.*

*Forgive, forget, release, let go,*
*all stressful discontent.*
*And be assured amidst the trial,*
*to rest upon His strength.*

*Possess the fullness of His love,*
*and cherish routes unknown.*
*For in the storm and through the flood,*
*you will not be alone.*

*To know, to stay, to fight, to prove,*
*to rest unchanged and calm,*
*Uncertain times, and tests of will,*
*can't shake His peaceful balm.*

## Chapter VI

# SOME MORNINGS ARE DARKER THAN OTHERS BUT IT'S STILL MORNING

dawn, daybreak, beginning, prime,
1st or early period of anything

*For His anger is but for a moment, but*
*His favor is for a lifetime.*
*Weeping may endure for a night, but joy*
*comes in the morning (Psalms 30:5).*

*"Morning is the mystery to the beginning of infinity"*
*James Lee Griffin Sr.*

*Injury to an athlete is more grueling*
*than the actual pain attached to*
*any previous training received. To consider*
*never playing again is torture.*
*Sitting out from practice, while recuperating*
*from surgery, seems like a life sentence.*

*The tendons and ligaments have to heal as the muscles recover. Then the painful process of reconditioning the body begins. Yes, those mornings are dark but persistence will break forth as daylight replaces the uncertainty.*

One morning, as I got into my car preparing to drive to work, I noticed that although it was 6:24am it was still very dark outside. The thought came to me that some mornings are darker than others but it is still morning. The sun is still as bright but we can only see it through the atmosphere and the elements that are closest to us. Through rain clouds, fog, smog, snow, or sleet, the light will break forth again.

Our mornings are subject to the lens
that we are looking through:
Joy or Sorrow
Optimism or Pessimism
A Half Full Glass or A Half Empty Glass
Healing or Pain
Faith or Doubt
Hope or Despair
Wisdom or Ignorance
A Pleasant Disposition or A Nasty Attitude
Unlimited Forgiveness or Debilitating Unforgiveness
Love or Hate
Impartiality or Prejudice
Compassionate or Critical
Liberal or Selfish
A Team Player or To Have it Your Way
To Be Reconciled or To Be Right

Six years ago, I felt the leading of the Lord to assist with the care of my elderly parents. My initial plans were to only spend one summer in Illinois, but phase one of this assignment lasted for three years.

This assignment was very challenging at first. My mother was very independent and use to taking care of herself. My initial presence on the scene was not very welcoming. And many mornings were darker than usual as I attempted to actively engage in my assignment to care for them both.

I remember sitting in the living room asking the Lord to lead and guide me where I should begin this journey. Discerning the path of least resistance, I began to clean the shelves that housed all of her souvenir collectables. They were very dusty and affected my mom's asthma. I began at the front door of her apartment with a large bowl of soapy water. Strategically proceeding around the living room from left to right, I began to clean each one with care and precision. Some of them were broken and couldn't be repaired. With great effort and disclosure, I discarded them outside of the watchful eye of Willie M. Strong, my mother. For the repairable ones, I got some glue and reconnected some of the heads that had broken off. By the time, I had finished this first project, I received a reserved thank you, and I was trusted with other projects. I learned quickly to use wisdom by making her think that it was all her idea.

During the first year and a half, I cared for my mother and stepfather. My stepfather was recovering from a stroke quite successfully. Then we found out that he had blood clots in both lungs. Two weeks later after the diagnosis, he went home to be with the Lord at the age of eighty-six. We experienced great joy because he accepted Christ as Savior in August, and transitioned two months later in October 2011. We miss him, but our sorrow has turned into joy at the delight that we will see Him again.

Fast forwarding to the present, while caring for my mother in Atlanta, she suffered a mild stroke four days after her eighty-seventh birthday. Frequent seizures and a deteriorating Alzheimer condition progressed quickly. Communication was challenging and it became very difficult to see her in that state. My prayer was that she would release all of her past hurts and be at total peace with Him. A calm and settling peace also engulfed me. With every nightly kiss, the ultimate presence of her destiny was evident. The "purpose of the Lord shall prevail" (Proverbs 19:21, Psalm 33:11). She peacefully transitioned at our home on September 22, 2016.

Capacity and compassion have been my personal tutors during this process. They have disclosed untapped and undiscovered resources that brought forth much fruit. To give of yourself yields great reward, unconditional love and so much more. My small sacrifice does not compare to the 100-fold blessings that I have already received.

Inspite of the temporary darkness, we must adjust
our situation to the action of the word. "Nay
in all these things*(Tests, Hurts, Il-Health,
Needs, Gloominess, Sadness),* we are more than conquerors.
Romans 8:37 It doesn't look or feel good, but good is
coming out of it! Yes, some mornings may be darker

than others, but the structure of the future is clear.
Walk through the darkness until the movement of its
winds changes your view of the future. Remember
now, "Morning is just one minute from midnight!"
*Dr. Beatrice Gardner*

**Walk through the Darkness to Win in the Morning!**

*Listen to the Leading*

*We must allow our heart to know*
*Within His presence His will can flow*
*To yield, respond, His grace abound*
*The voice of the Shepherd is so profound*

*His sheep will only follow the one*
*God sent from Heaven, Jesus Christ His Son*
*They know His voice, they know His call*
*They know His love for one and all*

*For God is not the author of confusion,*
*To those who wander this is an illusion.*
*Confusion, diversion, an adverse reaction,*
*The voice of a stranger is such distraction.*

*Elijah was the witness to a phenomenal occurrence,*
*No answer in the wind, earthquake, or fire,*
*such a terrible disturbance!*

*Choose to hear Him patiently*
*in His still small voice applaud.*
*So quiet yourself, be still and know,*
*that He alone is God.*

## Chapter VII
# LISTEN TO THE LEADING

To Hear…..
is to have the ability to receive sound vibrations.
To be informed of, to receive information

To Listen …..
is to attend, tune in, hearken, obey,
give attention to, give heed to,
give an audience to, respond to

*But he who listens to me shall live securely,*
*And will be at ease from the dread of evil (Proverbs 1:33).*

*He whose ear listens to the life-giving reproof,*
*will dwell among the wise (Proverbs 15:31).*

*"It is the province of knowledge to speak.*
*And it is the privilege of wisdom to listen".*
*Oliver Wendell Holmes 1805-1894*

*…Participants in team sports, learn to respond to the voice of their coaches. With extensive hours of instruction, the team*

*member develops a true connection and begins to think like the coach. Eventually, they respond to an inner voice which guides them through every ordeal as game strategies change…*

This spiritual walk is quite challenging at times. We have been trained and conditioned to think, reason, then respond to what is set before us. A lot of times our secular training to "TCB" (taking care of business), gets in the way of what the Lord is leading us to do. We have human ways to solutions and then there is "Godly wisdom," the ordained purpose driven way; how things should be done! The Holy Spirit is our guide in the earth but we must tap into His frequency to not only hear(register the audible vibrations) but to listen(give audience to and respond) to HIS leading.

Memphis, TN was my transitional place. This was my Jerusalem, my Mecca, my Damascus road, the place where my eyes were opened. Prior to this first relocation event, I had finally publically confessed Christ at eighteen, before leaving my hometown of Maywood, IL. With all of the negative press that follows a youth from the Chicago area, I desired to make a positive impact, rather than to be another negative statistic.

I completed my degree, which made my mom very proud, and then acquired a teaching position. After three years, and reaching tenure, my inner spirit felt a tug for something more. I did work in that position for two more years. With budget cuts and low enrollment, our school was slated for closure, and all the teachers were declared surplus. We were given the opportunity to apply for other teaching positions, but I felt the leading to travel and for full-time ministry. I was already teaching private lessons, so I increased by student roster, and played for churches for an additional two years. While waiting and praying for direction, an opportunity to travel as a musician unfolded, and the rest is history.

Now, what I didn't previously share with you was that I was met with major opposition from of course, my mother. By this time, I was a bit stronger in the word, and gleaned my courage and stability from the Lord. Our relationship was so strained that I was pressed to ask her a very daunting question. One day, I asked her, "Wouldn't you rather see me in the will of God, rather than on drugs or in the streets living any kind of way?" I reminded her that she was the one that took us to Sunday school as children, and taught us to love Jesus. Now, I was an adult, allowing Him to direct my entire life. He was leading me to do this. She didn't respond at all. She was quiet and never answered me.

This affected me to the point that I began to bombard the Lord with question after question. "Lord, why is she so against my decision? Haven't I sought your will in this for two more years now? Didn't I do everything she required of me? I stayed at home an extra year before going out of state to finished college? Didn't I become a teacher just like she wanted? Why can't she understand? And then, the clear, quiet response, from the Lord was, "I didn't tell her, I TOLD YOU!"

That was the only answer that I needed. I dried my tears and proceeded to prepare for the next assignment. And you must do the same! The bible says, "MY SHEEP", know MY voice, and a stranger they will not follow (John 10:4-5).

That very first encounter to listen to His leading opened the door to other opportunities to first "hear" the directive, but then to "listen," respond, and accomplish the task.

He is the one that doesn't lie.
He always tells you the truth.
(Numbers 23:19, Psalm 92:15, Malachi 3:6,
Titus 1:2, Hebrews 6:18, James 1:17-18)

My ways are not your ways,
and my thoughts are not your thoughts.
(Isaiah 55:8)

He will lead and guide us into all truth
(John 16:13)

**Win Your Race, By Listening to Respond!**

*To progress forward,*
*one must have a sense of what has been.*

*To progress onward,*
*one must release what is restricting the progression.*

*To stay focused,*
*one must determine truth from error.*

*To advance,*
*one must stay on course.*

## Chapter VIII
# CONDITIONING

To put in a fit or proper state
equip, sharpen, train, change the behavior of

*I appeal to you brothers, by the mercies of God to present your bodies a living sacrifice (Romans 12:1-2).*

"The conditioning process becomes beneficial only after one cooperates with: modification, adaptation, discomfort, and sometimes abrupt, life-altering, behavioral change."

*All athletic competitors, whether amateur or professional, will greatly benefit from conditioning training in four areas: High Intensity Interval Training, Aerobic Activity, Running Exercises, and Weight Training. The composite of these athletic tools builds endurance and stamina in all who will dare to fully engage in the above activities. Conditioning exercises build up, tone up, toughen up, and will whip you into shape. They will educate, train, and sharpen your athletic edge for success.*

By the time I reached my senior year in High School, there was no need to enlist in any U.S. Military branch of service. I had already gone through the "Strong Boot Camp". My entire formative years, had been lived with a live-in drill sergeant, and I had been forced to re-enlist for an extensive tour of duty in the "Strong" Institute of Special Services.

Since elementary school, conditioning had been a major part of my home training and my educational experience. My mother was the original creator of the term "*home school*" and made me read the dictionary every night since age six. I thought that she was the meanest mom in the world, but I never had a reading problem! Now, I read for others and another career quest is evolving for me; voice overs.

My sister and I changed schools quite a bit to benefit from better educational opportunities that were not available in our assigned area. With every move our socialization skills were developed. We were forced to acclimate to several unfamiliar environments, and to communicate with different types of people. This was my initial prep for the travel opportunities that would manifest later in my adult life.

Our extensive work resume began at age four. We were required to: recite speeches, participate in Christmas plays, serve as junior ushers and eventually play for Sunday school at age six. The list also included: piano, ballet, band, drama coaching, modeling, learning to sew, voice lessons for my sister, and organ lessons for me. Please remember this was in addition to our nightly homework assignments and special projects at school. We experienced life with a full plate and really didn't have time to get into trouble. The conditioning was very beneficial. When the time came to embrace career paths, we had many avenues to choose from.

The "Spiritual" Journey also serves as a conditioning tool; through preparation, equipping us by practice, modifying our inconsistency toward perseverance, and re-programming our responses, to the directives of the word. This type of conditioning will definitely educate and train you for the execution of your ordained assignment.

- High Intensity Interval Training-present your body a living sacrifice holy, acceptable unto God, which is your reasonable service (Romans 12: 1-2).
- Aerobic Activity-Put on the whole armor of God; belt of truth, breastplate of righteousness, feet fitted with the readincss of the gospel of peace, shield of faith, helmet of salvation, and sword of the Spirit, which is the word of God (Ephesians 6:13-17).
- Running Exercises- run and not be weary, walk and not faint (Isaiah 40:31).
- Weight Resistance Training-lay aside every weight (Hebrews 12:1):

*worry, doubt, impatience, stress, isolation, drought, sorrow, idols, lack,* and you fill in whatever I missed------------------------------------------.

Conditioning just like adjustments is not comfortable, but the rewards are great!

**Proceed Through The Conditioning Process to Win!**

## Summary

*"That day, I wept for the street that lead*
*me away and carried me back.*
*I wept for the process because it was worth the pain.*
*Then, I wept for the pain because I was*
*not use to the total absence of it"...*
*Henry & June;*
*The Diary of Anais Nin 1937-1934*

When we walk through our challenges we often wonder "why"? I've learned that even though we are the ones who actually tread through the trial, it is really for those who will be assigned to our route, after the process is complete.

Change is invoked from the inside. We can only effectively influence individuals who we are associated with in some way; face to face, email, text, Skype, internet, social media, e-books, sharing printed text, etc. A certain degree of trust and kinship are also necessary for the recipient to accept our transparency, while dealing with such sensitive areas of vulnerability.

My last teaching directive is very simple, yet profound:

Place more focus on the "***when***" part of the challenge
vs
the ***"why"*** part of the test....

"***When*** you go through deep waters, I will be with you.
***When*** you go through rivers of
difficulty, you will not drown.
***When*** you walk through the fire of
oppression, you will not be burned up;
the flames will not consume you" (Isaiah 43:2 NLT).

Make the Adjustment to **Win**!

Apply Courage to **Win**!

**Win** in Private to Prepare for Public Promotion!

**Win** While You Wait in Patience!

Walk through the Darkness to **Win** in the Morning!

**Win** Your Race by Listening to Respond!

Proceed Through The Conditioning Process to **Win**!

***Thank You for Sharing in My Journey to Win!***
*Tamara Lofton*

# About the Author

Tamara accepted the Lord as "Savior and Lord of her life" at age eighteen, but in reflection, she hadn't acknowledged Him about what her total career path should be. Coming from a lineage of educators, she also decided to be a teacher. Music was all that she knew; piano lessons since age four, played for churches since age twelve, trained choirs at age fifteen, went to college as a Music Ed major, studied voice, became a High School music teacher, wrote gospel songs and commercial jingles, and traveled for thirteen years as an organist for an evangelist.

She had chosen music, but He had another plan. Somewhere between learning to yield to His purpose, and doing life, something changed! The Lord breathed life into dormant gifts, using her in areas that she had not been professionally trained in. A love for music transitioned into a passion for the word. Basic reading, writing, math, and typing skills, became the catalyst. A genuine love for people surfaced. Her focus changed, and she connected, by becoming a tutor of music, math, and the message of Christ. An author and administrator was born, replacing the career path that she had previously chosen for herself.

Tamara is a member of New Covenant Christian Ministries in Lithonia, Ga. pastored by, Pastor Billy R. and Dr. D'Ann Johnson. She has served in several capacities; minister, worship & arts, voice over announcer, and facilitator for school of ministry, discipleship, and small groups classes.

*Contact the Author…*

Email:
*tamrhythmic@yahoo.com*

*Mailing Address:*
*P.O. Box 239*
*Stone Mountain, Ga 30086*

*Projects are Available in:*
*Soft Cover, E-Books, Audio Books*

*The Cost of the Win Part I*
*The Cost of the Win Part II*
*Saints Survival Kit*

*Projects in Audio Versions*
*Only:*
*Trust and Don't Trip*
*Your Temptation-Affected By It or Infected With It?*
*A Functioning Vessel or a Vessel of Purpose?*
*Study Tips from A to Z*

Printed in the United States
By Bookmasters